Printed in France by Amazon
Brétigny-sur-Orge, FR

16898900R00070